i

Poetry and Thoughts of a
Wandering Man
Uniquely Colorado Edition

Kurt James

DEDICATION

I would like to dedicate this book of poetry to those that have made my life more worthwhile as I have gotten older. Keegan and Conner are my grandkids and I love them both to the moon and back.

ACKNOWLEDGMENTS

Many thanks to R J Schwartz from Idaho and John Hansen from Australia who created Creative Exiles - a website to give the freedom of expression to some amazing poets from around the world.

Disclaimer

This is a work of poetry and not intended to be historical fact. Names, characters, businesses, places, events and incidents are either the products of the author's imagination or history as the author understands it.

Kurt James

TABLE OF CONTENTS

Ghost Train

Living at the base of the Rocky Mountains all my life I have learned even in the most remote wilderness areas that they are not as empty or silent as they appear. There is not an old cemetery, town, horse trail, mountain pass, or railroad tunnel that does not have an old story or two to tell from days gone by in the Colorado Rockies or the surrounding states. These remote mountains I have learned have ghost tales that are best told on a cold autumn night with friends and family around a shimmering campfire as the mountain wind tickles the aspen trees to begin their autumn melody of the tree whispers. This is one of those tales. True or not - it is a tale of a ghost train that rides the rails just beyond the Moffat Tunnel east of Rollins Pass, Colorado. I do not recall how or even the circumstances of how I heard this ghost tale, but this haunting story of the ghost train I have never forgotten.

"Ghost Train"

In the distance blinding light appeared,
Bone chilling, silent, and to be feared.
Stroke of 12, out of the dark night it came,
Railroad tracks and metal wheels aflame.
Engine of steam bellowing misty white smoke,
Ghost train, Hell on Wheels going for broke.
Blowing white steam, sparks of fire close to me,
Death the conductor, waving a skeleton key.
Black railroad cars packed full of pasty face folks,
No smiles, just tears, no happiness for these blokes.
Specter of Death, looked at me with a ghastly smile,
Skull with hollow sockets gazed at me for half a mile.
How and where it came from, I will never be able to tell,
All I know, Ghost train passengers going straight to Hell.

Silver Heels

Colorado is full of old ghost towns, mines, rugged mountain passes, and trails that have long been forgotten - vanished like the dust in the wind. Some of the old tales of the mountain frontier remain and in the retelling become legends. Boreas Pass is a trail that connects the old ghost town of Como to Breckenridge, Colorado. Near the top of this pass and if you look to the south there is a mountain peak named Mount Silver Heels. This mountain is a reminder of a legend that folks there in the mountains still speak of.

3

"Silver Heels"

In the Buckskin Joe gold camp, she arrived by way of the
Denver to Fairplay stage,
Exquisitely dressed in a long black dress - no one could guess
her age.
She was inescapably beautiful, petite, quint, with raven colored
hair,
Lifting her dress above the snow and mud, she seemed to dance
in the air.
Gold miners, freighters, and men of the mountain were taken in
by the girl,
As she stepped up to the boardwalk and gave her parasol a
suggestive twirl.
Among the soiled doves she became the "Fancy Lady" in Bill
Bucks dance hall,
In the loneliness of the mountain winter snow – she won the
hearts of them all.
In this gold camp of Buckskin Joe in the Colorado high
mountains so remote,
The local newspaper it appeared - "The coming of an Angel" –
someone wrote.
Her real name remained a mystery – there were rumors, but no
one ever knew

Adorned in tight-fitting satin gowns and silver heels – the miners love for her only grew.
It was the girl's shiny silver heels that would give her the immortal nickname,
Back then and forever in those isolated mountains - "Silver Heels" – she became.
With a vengeance in the fall of 1861 another visitor came to Buckskin Joe,
Extremely painful, debilitating, and disfiguring – "Smallpox" - put on a show.
Death and disease was about to devastate the mining town of Buckskin Joe,
During those cold and desolate days and months of the autumn and winter snow.
Amid the heartbreak, disease, and death, that the Silver Heels' legend would be made.
She cared for the sick and dying from cabin to cabin – heaven sent and never afraid.
She held the sick miners and comforted them risking her only asset – her beauty,
Songs and dance were lost in the panic – caring for those in need became her duty.
In the final hours of the epidemic – tragically – Silver Heels would catch the disease,
As the last of the sick – she was carried to her cabin down by the river and the trees.
In her isolated cabin Silver Heels declined deep into delirium and the darkness,
Smallpox had all but vanished from Buckskin Joe, but still proved forever heartless
As the gold miners, children, women, and the town, healed and returned to what was,
Silver Heels, pockmarked, her beauty gone and would nevermore hear the applause.

Grateful miners gathered a purse of five thousand dollars for
Silver Heels all in gold,
When they went to her cabin – she was gone – vanished – or so
the legend is told.
Some say for numerous years following the smallpox epidemic
of Buckskin Joe,
In the cemetery a mysterious veiled woman wearing a satin
gown, silver heels – forever strolls.

Mountain Folk

When photographing and exploring the Colorado Mountains
you come to realize that the folks that live in the remote high
country are sort of – let's say different. They normally are folks for
reasons of their own really don't like people so they chose to
distance themselves from folks like you and me. They will tolerate
us for a short spell, but they really would rather be by themselves.
They are and always will be the "Mountain Folk."

"Mountain Folk"

You will learn in the mountains of Colorado – the folks are a
different breed,
Some are city rejects, some were mountain natural born – all
from a peculiar seed.
It is not the resorts or the big cities that the "mountain folk"
live and reside,
But, the near ghost towns like Como, Russell Gulch, and Alma
– live the certified.
Sort of comes naturally to make fun of those that live near the
timberline high,
Been my experience – the thinner air makes their brain pans
go slightly awry.
Mountain folk usually are as nervous as a cat in a room full of
rockers,
When lost – and ask directions – you will find they are not a
lot of talkers.
Finding a helpful mountain folk – is almost guaranteed it will
be a long shot.

If you do get a talker, they mumble, "Don't go gettin' your knickers in a knot."
Sure enough, they will point you down the road as they give you a lot of crap,
Spitting – then mutter, "You couldn't find your ass with both hands and a map"
In the high timber I have seen mountain folk that would make coffee nervous,
Just a few minutes with the mountain folk – sure enough will leave you wordless.
God forbid if you happen to run your Jeep or 4-wheeler into a mountain ditch,
Along comes a mountain folk in a rusty truck – grumbling, "Gaul darn sum bitch."
If you cuss a mountain folk they will stomp a mud hole in your ass and walk it dry,
Mountain folk gets meaner, off- kilter, and crazier the closer you get to the sky.
I know what has floated across your braincase, "He's nuttier than a squirrel turd."
You will have to excuse me – the thin mountain air here has my thinker blurred.

Alfred Packer

Then There Was Only One – Growing up in Denver, Colorado at the foot of the Rocky Mountains during the 60's and 70's you would at some time hear the tale of - "Alfred G. Packer" - Colorado cannibal. It is a chilling tale of wilderness survival of some gold prospectors that were lost in the rugged mountain wilderness of the Rocky Mountains near Lake City, Colorado. Six men entered the remote winter wilderness and only one would survive to walk out several months later. Alfred was buried in the Littleton Cemetery not far from my childhood home. This is my version of the tale of the Colorado Cannibal.

"Alfred Packer"

Bitter cold winter, Colorado 1874,
Alfred Packer - became campfire lore.
Breckenridge gold fields they had in mind,
Alfred and five others - the yellow dust had blind.
On the Gunnison River the Ute Indian Chief Ouray,
Feared Packer's and crew of five would become winters prey.
"Never to fear" - Alfred Packer was heard to say,
Headed into the San Juan's on a freezing winter day.
On a remote mountain Plateau - snowbound they became,
Not gold or silver, but survival now was the ultimate game.
Flesh freezing winter cold, became more intense,
Out of food and provisions – only increased the suspense.
Now only one man knows the truth of what happened in this tale,
Alfred Packer – the lone survivor – survived the wilderness trail.
Out of the winter perdition, not much out of sort,
Five others lives and dreams had fallen deadly short.
Now how did Packer – one man survive the winter Hell?
People of Lake City, Colorado did not believe his tale.
During a winter struggle with no provisions or food,
That Alfred Packer lived – looked healthy and renewed.

Widely believed with hatchet their heads he did split,
And ate the other five – flesh cooked on a campfire spit.
Over a hundred years later, if it is this legend you seek,
Near Lake City, Colorado, is a mountain named – Cannibal
Peak.

Broken Dreams

We all have dreams and when I was 10 years old mine centered on - becoming a mountain man like my heroes of old or playing football for the Denver Broncos. -From that first moment in time that we can form our own thoughts – we start to dream of better things for our future. Living life to the fullest is all about the quest to follow our hearts desires and dreams of what will be. Some of us in this human condition only think that our lives are accomplished if we set out and achieve whatever dreams you have dangled in front of yourself like the proverbial "carrot on a stick." The truth of the matter is that more likely than not you will fall short of achieving that much sought after dream. For whatever reason – be it your fault or simply fate we fall short of completing and achieving them – and your dream becomes shattered and broken. I would like to suggest to you – the reader that - dreams are made to be broken. Living life to the end of our existence is not about achieving those dreams. If you do, the world is yours, but if you don't the world still is yours. The key is not the end result of those dreams, but the quest and everything in between is what life is all about. So when a dream becomes broken – do not despair – find another and dream again.

13

"Broken Dreams"

Down through my life cemented in my past,
Broken dreams scattered - pieces of shattered glass.
Some dreams were never truly meant to be,
Some broken dreams were meant - to set me free.
Cannot break me, a lifetime of broken dreams,
I am willing and stronger than most or so it seems.
From my past - broken dreams that cannot break me,
Not jaded, and daring to dream again is the key.
My broken dreams are not the end of the road,
For another dream comes along - waiting to be saddled and
rode.
Broken dreams can mean life has a new direction,
For a new acquired dream for my reflection.

Moon Whisper

Moon Whisper is nothing new. The Ute Indians of the Colorado Rocky Mountains, believed that the moon could speak to them. Man has always been fascinated by the ancient moon down through the ages, but growing up it also had a special meaning to me. Even as a small child, I was captivated by it, the moon and all its mystery spoke directly to me – or so I believed. It has always been my friend and ally when I had none. This romantic notion I have with the moon has never left me as I have grown older. As a wildlife and nature photographer, I take every opportunity I can to take photos of the moon and its whispers. As a writer of western adventure novels you can be assured that my stories have an element of the moon mystery and wonders somewhere in the story. This poem is for any of you that have heard the – Moon Whisper.

"Moon Whisper"

The moon when I was little it would listen to me,
As I laid outdoors under the old evergreen tree.
Never judged me it always remained silent in the night,
Telling my secrets to the moon above only seemed right.
Blue, or yellow - the color of the moon didn't matter much,
The moon knew all my childhood fears, mysteries and such.
It always knew my misery when my father had too much to
drink,
When in the dark I would find solace with the moon - it lets
me think.
Of course the moon knew of the pigtailed girl down the street,
As I kissed her on the kiddie swing and told me I was sweet.
When I was young I use to think the moon was only for me,
High in the heavens; on earth I was the only one it could see.
The moon above knew all my thoughts, hopes, and dreams,
All my expectations, visions, and imaginings rode those
moons beams.
When I was little the moon was more than my friend high in
the sky,
It helped me with my struggles and fears – it was my ally.
Sometimes, as I have gotten older I lose touch with my moon,
When that happens, I look heavenward and get my life back in
tune.
The moon when I was little it would listen to me,
As I laid outdoors under the old evergreen tree.

Nevadaville

Colorado has numerous tales of those that lived and died along the Rocky Mountain frontier. As a young boy I was fascinated by such tales of gold camps, ghost towns, Ute Indians, outlaws, miners, marshals, gamblers, and soiled doves that made those stories come alive to me. Even as a young boy I wanted to walk the trails, explore the mountains of those that walked these mountains of old before me. Nevadaville, Colorado is one ghost town that I have spent plenty of time exploring since it was roughly 45 minutes from my boyhood home. Even to this day when I visit that lonely town on Bald Mountain I still feel the chills of the ghost's that still reside there. Come with me – let's take a stroll.

"Nevadaville"

Nevadaville, Colorado, empty buildings, silent streets,
Death knell that rang out in this town, now complete.
As I walk the boardwalk's of Nevadaville today,
I feel ghostly eyes of yesteryear follow me from fading doorways.
When I close my eyes - I can hear the sounds of so long ago,
Sounds of horses, spectral voices, mixed in with a distant banjo.
Stale whiskey, horse manure, sweat, and outhouse's still in use,
All these phantom scents in this town are still on the loose.
I stop and wonder of the lives that had lived here,
Of folks long gone, dead and buried –which brings a tear.
Memories of those erased by the wind and the dust,
Hopes, dreams, a silent death, when the gold went bust.
Graves on Bald mountain, cemetery tombstones due west,
Those unfortunate souls who died giving it their very best.
Now years later, nature tries to claim its right, its own,
Buildings, boardwalks degrade into the unknown.

Dirty Annie

This poem is an ode to Annabelle Stark also known as "Dirty Annie" of Saint Elmo, Colorado – part of living in Colorado and exploring the Rocky Mountains are the old tales of yesteryear. Every Colorado small mountain town has its tales of broken hearts, lost gold and treasure, outlaws, miners, soiled doves and of course - ghosts. I have always loved a good ghost story. Saint Elmo is a real ghost town on the east side of Tin Cup Pass that during the winter, it is not accessible due to heavy and deep snow. During the spring and summer it is much traveled for those that dare to 4-wheel over the rugged pass. During the autumn it is a must see for the autumn wonders of the leaves changing. If you live in Colorado and have ever made the trip you need to know the story of "Dirty Annie".

"Dirty Annie"

She walks out of the shadows when the day turns dark,
Saint Elmo's only full time resident is Annabelle Stark.
From the hotel window overlooking the Stark family store,
Watching the empty boardwalks of Saint Elmo once more.
She was born, raised, lived and breathed - this was her town,
Never thought of leaving even when the gold mines shut
down.
When young Annie was beautiful, and the talk of the town,
Many years later she would have her mental breakdown.
"Dirty Annie" a nickname given as she grew older and aged,
Never bathing and tangled hair as mental illness raged.
Known to patrol the dusty streets with a pistol and shotgun,
Year in and year out as her afflicted mind became undone.
"Dirty Annie's" hotel deteriorated as well as the family store,
Trash and sour smelling food tins began to pile up on the
floor.
In the year of our Lord 1960 "Dirty Annie" fell ill and she
died,
Some say at night in Saint Elmo that her ghost still resides.

Tree Whispers

Being a child of Colorado and growing into a man of nature, there is nothing more pleasing and comforting than listening to the sound the aspen leaves make when the wind blows across the mighty Rocky Mountains. Walking these mountains of old I always become enchanted with what I call the "Tree Whispers." Those songs and melodies brought forth from the mountain winds are meant to be cherished by the few who stop and take a moment and really listen. No orchestra or string quartet – though lovely – can match the "Tree Whispers." Numerous times while walking with someone through my mountains and the aspen groves I will stop and say "Do you hear that?" More often than not they will stop along with me and turn their ear, and reply, "No, did you hear something?" Most of modern man is not in tune with nature or the trees. They simply are on a path to get somewhere, never realizing it is not the end of the path that is the quest – but, what we see, feel, or hear that is important along that path. We all need to take a minute out of our day and really stop and feel, see, and listen to the glory of nature that surrounds us. How sad it is that most never take that minute. As a child I use to think that the "Tree Whispers" only spoke and sang their hexing melody to me. As a grown man of the mountain I know this not to be true. But, I wonder – if you can hear them too?

"Tree Whispers"

When the wind builds from the north,
The silence is broken, trees whispers comes forth.
Wind, the rustle all becomes music to me,
Nature's song drifts down from the whisper tree.
Standing alone in the chilled air I breathe,
Nature is my auditorium as the music seethes.
Chilled wind slowly dies, tree whispers no more,
Walking away from the trees – and that whisper song I adore.

Summer Creek

My Summer Creek - was named Bear Creek and it was roughly three blocks from my childhood home in Sheridan, Colorado. I miss those times of yesteryear - mostly I miss my summers on Bear Creek. Little did my friends and I know that those memories we made on those hot summer days would walk with us through the rest of our lives. One of my most profound memories of my summer creek was one year my friends all happened to be on family vacations at the same time leaving me all alone on the bank of Bear Creek. I was far from lonely that summer as I sat in the high grass with my feet dangling in the cool flowing water of Bear Creek, because I discovered new friends and they kept me entertained that summer. My new friends were writers like H. G. Wells, Louis L'Amour, Jules Verne, and Edgar Rice Burrows. These men, these strangers somehow knew what I needed that summer while my friends were away and I was never lonely in between the pages of their stories. Yes, a big portion of my wonder years was centered on my summer creek.

"Summer Creek"

Now I am a lot older and far away,
I remember, the summers that started in May.
Down to the banks of old Bear Creek,
Young lad dreams, adventures, we would seek.
Bear Creek was not wide, not deep, not swift,
Perfect to give us tykes a summer lift.
We tubed, we swam, and we would wade,
We, as young boys, had it made.
Caught sunburns more than rainbow trout,
Somehow that was what it was all about.
Timeless friends, best of, we were all,
Splashing, dunking, until we would hear our Mothers call.
Going home when day turned to night,
Returning the next day, at early dawn light.
Now I am older and far away,
Smile when I think of young summer days.

"Windows of the Past"

Since my early attempts of photography using the original Polaroid Instamatic camera I have been fascinated with the power of photography. Looking at old photos of your family can have and leave an emotional impact on you, as you view slices of time from your past. As a youngster, I would read science-fiction about time travel and longed for the day that it would be possible. I would come to realize it was already possible with the power and magic of windows of the past. Often some photos give you a glimpse of how your relatives lived and did things before you were born. They never knew that the photos that were being taken would in time become viewed by those that never knew them, but never less loved them. I know for me that viewing these shared memories in old black and white and sepia that were most of the time grainy, and out of focus, but, have always been a treat for me to travel down a forgotten path. At the end of life, it really is just memories that we leave behind in the ones we love. Leave behind a photo or two to help those remember you. Travel the roads of yesteryear and go find that old shoe box or dusty album of family photos so you can smile or cry, of those that made you what you are today.

"Windows of the Past"

Just the other day I found them among the dust and the mold,
Images of long ago, sifting through - my history began to
unfold.
An old cardboard shoebox full of tiny windows of the past,
Pulling the top off in the swirling dust, "What do I have here"
– I asked.
Long lost treasure of my family in sepia, and black and white,
At the top of the box, forgotten and dusty memories suddenly
came to light.
Photos looked back at me, reminded me who I loved and when
they passed,
Emotion back and forth, remembering when I saw them last.
One moment sadness would overcome me and eyes fill with
tears,

To be replaced suddenly with happiness I felt down through
the years.
Grandparents, uncles, aunts and cousins, some still with me, I
must make a call,
Deeper into the box were photos of the ones passed that I
never knew at all.
Thankfully, I now have in possession my treasure box of
hidden family gold,
Grateful that I was able to save it from the swirling dust and
thicken mold.

The Window

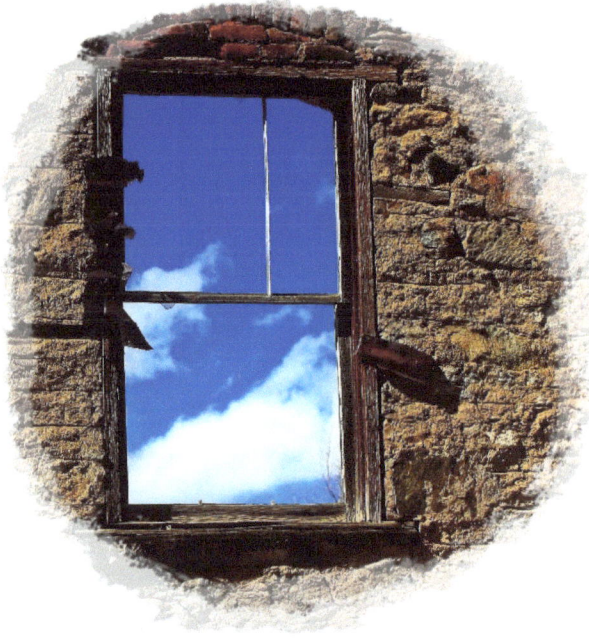

As I wander through the Rocky Mountains and the forgotten ghost towns and cemeteries of days gone by, I have taken thousands of photographs. Some I like right away and after a little work I post them on social media and for sale – most I store for viewing later. Every once in a while I will review one and I am like, "How did I miss that one the first go around?" Others like the one above jump out at me and tell their own story – I view - and I listen to the story the photo has to tell. Pull up a log to my campfire and here is the story I heard.

"The Window"

She never liked it when her husband gave her the pitch,
About heading to the gold camps out west to make them rich.
Day after day she never left the window out of fear,
Hoping that she would glimpse her love as he got near.
Winter, summer, autumn, and spring all came and went,
He never sent word – she could not fathom what it meant.
Her hours turned into days – then months – then years,
It had become so long her eyes could no longer find the tears.
Sitting silently at the bay window year after year,
Waiting for her husband the one she loved – to reappear.
Feeling their mother's misery – her children now grown,
Never leaving the window – her mind in a dark abyss – and all
alone.
Sitting out the window in time she aged and grew old,
Waiting for her husband – her – their story ending to unfold.
Her home aged - crumbled to the weather and the rust,
At the window, she died and returned to whence she came –
the dust.
After she died and years later when the wind is out of the
west,
Still sitting – just a shadow of herself still waiting her ghostly
quest.

Colorado Autumn

As I have grown older I have never lost my wonder of the four seasons that we experience in my native state of Colorado. I enjoy all four of the seasons, but autumn is my favorite. There is a part of me that will always want to walk amongst the autumn leaves as they glide back and forth in their bid to find their final resting place before the first snow. It is the harmony of the season that appeals to me, not too hot and not too cold. You can smell the wood smoke from the chimneys in the neighborhood as the kids and dogs play hide and seek using the red, gold, orange and brown leaves as cover. I feel sorry for those that do not take the time to look to the west at a Colorado autumn with its orange and red sunset in all its grandeur in the chilled night air. The coldness of the air seems to draw the colors out and make them more exquisite and pleasing to the eye. I do not believe I would be happy in a world without Colorado Octobers.

"Colorado Autumn"

More than half a century Colorado autumns I have seen,
Never once has autumn in October to me ever been routine.
Even as a child - autumn has always been my favorite time of
year,
Those colorful months before winter kicked into high gear.
Chilled air and leaves falling almost silent in the path I walk,
End of summer - start of winter - the seasons interlock.
Mountains and valleys - autumn leaves are now aflame,
As a misty chilled autumn breeze lays its rightful claim.
Rivers and streams - flowing water crisp and clear,
Sounds of the autumn tree whispers breathe upon my ear.
Days become shorter, the nights become longer,
Cool autumn breeze gets stronger and stronger.
Elk coats become prime - when developing their winter thick,
As ole' man winter extinguishes the autumn candle wick.
As I walk the path of autumn life of fifty plus years,
Behind me - almost silent autumn leaves make it disappear.

Shadows

When I was young there was never anything I looked more forward to than camping in the high wilderness of the Rocky Mountains of Colorado. During the day I was a mountain man, a mighty and fearless warrior in nature. I fished, climbed trees, and explored old forgotten ghost towns. I would also look for lost treasure, and learned the ends and outs of surviving in the sometimes harsh environment near and above timberline. I was the typical kid that loved anything and everything about my Rocky Mountains. Except one thing – the shadows. As the sun would dip into the western horizon, my old and ancient enemy - the shadow and his brothers would start to make their appearance. As the light started to fade my foe would gain strength as the vestiges become longer and more menacing as they advanced from the evergreen and aspen trees that they had been hiding in as the sun dipped down behind them. There was nothing worse in my mind than getting caught away from the camp and the safety of the campfire when the apparitions started to appear. I have always had a vivid imagination and the phantasms knew how to play on my fears. They knew my weakness like no other, even today when spending time in the woods, I think of those days when I feared the shadows. Maybe, just maybe I still fear them a little.

"Shadows"

Darkness of the night - the hour is late,
Shadows begin their dance and start to skate.
Full moon hidden behind dark clouds,
Shadows start to creep - ever growing dark shrouds.
Darkening shadows speak of increasing doom,
Swear the mountain air chilled as cold as a tomb.
As a young lad, learned about shadows - beware,
Nothing stops them - not even the Lord's Prayer.
Apparitions jump from tree to tree,
As darkness and shadows begin to circle me.
Lost in the woods and vestiges to be feared,
Distance, in the distance an orange glow did appear.
Faster and faster as I approached the flickering light,
Shadows falling behind, during this dark moonless night.
Voices, laughter, the smell of a campfire,
Closer to the fire, the shadows begin to expire.

Telluride

I am a native Coloradan and have traveled and seen more of the United States than most people in my life. In my humble opinion, there is no place more breathtaking beautiful than the Dallas Divide of the spur of the mighty Rocky Mountains called the San Juan Mountains. Telluride can be found there. What is unique about Telluride is that you cannot drive through it - you can only drive to it. It is the end of the road and the backdrop is something you will have never seen anywhere else in the world.

The town itself is nestled in the serenity of the San Juan's Mountains. I have tried to make the 6 hour drive ever year from my home in Loveland, Colorado in the middle of October during autumn to capture nature's handiwork between Ridgway, Colorado and Telluride, Colorado. My short poem does not do justice to what one can view. If you or anyone you know gets a chance to visit my state during autumn – tell them Kurt James said, "Go to Telluride, Colorado and he promises you that you will never want to leave." I love Colorado, I love the people, and I love my mountains.

"Telluride"

A longing came over me, I must abide
Loaded my pickup for the trip to Telluride
The lord created the earth, but saved it for last
Dallas Divide, marrow of the Earth, he cast
Serenity, happiness there does not elude me,
Among the San Juan Mountains as far as I can see
Nothing created in the world can overshadow
Majestic mountain beauty of Telluride, Colorado

TELLURIDE

Kurt James

Woman in Black

Some of us never question the existence of ghosts and others laugh off such stories as utter nonsense. What do I believe? In the daylight hours with the sun high in the sky, I do not believe in such tales, but when darkness falls and a full moon is overhead I am much more open minded. Of course I have spent all my wonder years walking the Colorado Rocky Mountains, which are older than time. I have hiked down the forgotten boardwalks of long lost mining towns and the overgrown mislaid cemeteries that dot the back roads of my mountains. I have spent countless hours reading the epitaphs of those folks that lived and died on windblown tombstones and rotted crosses. Ghosts in the end may not be real, but one thing that I have felt in my bones and my soul is the human misery of such places. "Woman in Black" is my version of a ghost story that may or may not haunt the streets of Central City, Colorado.

"Woman in Black"

Walking bundled up against the night, cold and snow,
Quarter size snowflakes floated in the streetlights glow.
She appeared dressed in black, with button up shoes,
Across the street veiled by falling snow looking confused.
Looking the part of this rustic mountain mining town,
Woman out of time looking at me, no smile - just a frown.
Pacing the street up and down, this way and that,
Panicked look I could see below her glistening black fur hat.
Slowly crossing the street in the wet slush and snow,
Now next to her, noticing her face had an eerie pale glow.
Sadness was upon her face as she looked at me,
As the snow got thicker, she was harder for me to see.
With a mournful look - she reached for me as she began to
fade,
In the darkness before me now - only snowflakes swayed.
Confused staring in the dark and the snow on the ground,
My footprints only, hers were nowhere to be found.
Slowly I walked away, turning my collar to the cold and
damp,
I knew I had seen the - "woman in black " - ghost in this old
mining camp.

Graves Forgotten

Born and raised in the state of Colorado, I have spent considerable time wandering these ancient mountains. It isn't just the beauty of nature that brings me back time after time. I have always been drawn to the tales of those who lived and died in the Rocky Mountain frontier long before I ever stepped foot in the mountains. Scattered throughout the Rockies are the lonely and lost cemeteries of graves forgotten with the passage of time. One of my favorite quotes is by the naturalist John Muir, who simply said "The Mountains are calling, so I must go." Those that are buried in the graves forgotten just as I have – heard that call of the mountains – and just like me they followed it. As I walk amongst the wooden crosses and tombstones with camera in hand, I sometimes become overwhelmed with emotion after reading the sad stories of some of the epitaphs on the graves forgotten. Just a word or short phrase that marks that a person that had hopes, dreams, and failures was buried there and that they use to walk the earth as a mortal being. It is evident from my walks among the dead that those that braved the high adventure of the Colorado Mountains in those frontier years died an early death. The mountains, they learned are callous, hard, and not very forgiving. At any given moment, sometimes I feel the need to reach out and touch a wooden cross or long forgotten tombstone and I can feel the energy tingle in my hand and arm of those that have passed. I know then and only then that their physical story ended here in the dirt under my feet, but their spiritual life has not ceased. I am not sure what to think of that.

"Graves Forgotten"

Lonely are the ones, graves forgotten,
Cemetery signs are gone, wood has rotten.
Tombstones tilted and grass has gone to seed,
Darkness falls and mournful wails - simply plead.
We loved and were loved before we died,
Forget us not - for eternity here we reside.
Rain, snow, autumn leaves have rotten,
Lonely are the ones, graves forgotten.

Sad tale of Clifford Griffin

I for one hear and listen to the music of the Colorado Rocky Mountains. The wind that causes the trees to whisper, raindrops on aspen leaves, the hoot of a faraway owl – all of this is music to me. Sometimes high on the mountain of the towns that the glory has left, you hear the music of those that once were. The music of all that ghost has always left me sad. Here now is such a tale.

"Sad tale of Clifford Griffin"

Silver Plume and Clifford Griffin – oh' what a sad tale indeed,
Even years later in the retelling – tragic – listen, but take heed.
Clifford was an eastern man born wealthy with a silver spoon,
When he asked his love for her hand in marriage one rainy
afternoon.
The young bride was beautiful and enchanted – or so it
seemed,
Clifford was handsome, and affluent – more than she had
dreamed.
Blissful they were – wedding plans were made for the bride
and groom,
Not knowing that fate and death waited outside in the wet and
gloom.
The night before their nuptials the young lady became sick
and died,
Death had taken his lady love – the woman that was to be his
bride.
For three days he held her lifeless body – Clifford's heart now
broken,
Through the tears and grief those many hours he remained
unspoken.

His grief and misery from her death would forever be proven
timeless.
Through anguished and despair – Clifford a good man never
lost his kindness.
Hoping to forget what he thought should be – and death's long
shadow,
With his forever love now gone, he fled west to Silver Plume,
Colorado.
Located at the base of Pendleton Mountain and below
timberline,
Clifford in Colorado became the owner not of a gold, but, a
silver mine.
History, and his miners would always say he was one hell of a
boss,
Even though sorrow and the death of his love would be his
albatross.
Sundays and every day at the end of his employees and miners
shift,
Clifford alone in his silver mine – played a violin – music was
his gift.
Above the town the sad music, and melancholy would drift on
down,
Clifford used his violin, bow, and music – his misery he tried
to drown.
Sitting on their porches and listening to the mournful music –
the miners would,
Knowing his tale they thought the music made him happy –
they misunderstood.
For several years, this was Clifford's unhappy life as it was
meant to be,
One night he thought of a solution that he thought would set
him free.
On this night the music played for longer than any night
before,
Until midnight the music honored the love and the one he
adored.
At the stroke of midnight – mountains echoed the sound of a
gunshot,

Clifford took his own life against the one and only demon he
fought.
The miners found him – pistol still in his hand – violin at his
side,
As he entered the afterlife to be with his love – his almost
bride.
A hundred years or more have passed since the tale of Clifford
Griffin,
He still plays his violin and the sad music – you only have to
listen.
Some sad songs and stories of love – beyond this life they
transcend,
In Silver Plume, Colorado is where Clifford's heartbreaking
tale never ends.

"If tears could build a stairway,
And memories a lane,
I'd walk right up to Heaven
And bring you home again."
—Unknown

Jim Cameron

In 1977 and being a child of the Rocky Mountains, my friends and I would spend every free moment four wheeling, and exploring what was our backyard. There was no ghost town or mountain pass that we had not set foot in within a 3 hour drive from our home in Sheridan, Colorado. We wanted to be mountain men and the girls loved it when we traveled to our nearby Rockies. Central City was an old gold mining town and only a 45 minute drive and we spent considerable time exploring the high mountains surrounding it. On one such trip just before sundown as we watched another glorious mountain sunset a man and his dog walked out of the woods. He was grizzled and gray and walked with a limp, his dog was not in much better shape than the old man. We invited him for a supper of roasted hot dogs with all the fixings and he seemed grateful for the meal as was his dog. We worried about him being so far into the remote mountains with the darkness now upon us, we fixed him and his dog a bedroll for the night. That night around the campfire watching the glowing orange and red embers float to the heavens. The old man told us a ghost tale and swore he himself had seen the ghost. We had no reason to doubt the old man as he told the tale of the ghost of Jim Cameron. The next morning after telling of the tale he vanished as if he or his dog were never there. This is how I remember it.

44

"Jim Cameron"

Jim Cameron died November 1st, 1887,
Death called that dark night at the hour of 11.
His mortal remains were buried in Masonic Cemetery,
The days became years, what came next is legendary.
Every year, on that day at the stroke of 11 she appears out of a shadow,
On the lonely hilltop north of Central City Colorado.
Dressed in an ebony felt hat and a black satin dress,
How she knew him, who she was, no one could guess.
Button up shoes drift above the mountain grass,
Floating through the aspens to Jim's tombstone at last.
No footprints in the dew on the grass or the soft ground,
Nor wind in the trees or hoot of an owl, nothing - no sound.
The air became frosty and chilled in a sudden cold wave,
As the woman in black hovered above Jim's grave.
I moved for a closer look through the still and chilled air,
Her shimmering eyes seemed to speak "How do you dare?"
Minutes turned into an hour, just at the caress of midnight,
Looking at me with melancholy eyes, she faded out of sight.
My mind was trying to make sense what I had just viewed,
Feeling sad and guilty for it was not my place to intrude.

Lady in Green

If one wanted to see the "Lady in Green" you would have to head to the eastern plains of Fort Laramie, Wyoming to an old army fort that has been left to weather the winter snow and the hot summer heat. It is a ghost tale told by many of those windswept plains just an hour north of Colorado. Just like the old west, which has faded into the past, so have all the ghosts of those that lived in those exciting and adventurous times. Although some of the tales have been lost to the passages of time, some of the old tales and stories still linger. Some of the ghosts still walk or ride the earth for evermore. Even if you do not believe, the child in you wants to believe. Pull up a log and sit down to my campfire for I have a tale for you

"Lady in Green"

This is a tale of a young Lady in Green,
Riding horseback, never more to be seen.
Fort Laramie, plains of Eastern Wyoming,
1871, Indians not tame - bands were roaming.
Daughter of the Sutler, his store within the fort,
Rode her horse outside the walls without an escort.
Dressed in a riding habit of emerald green,
Beautiful girl with eyes of blue and seventeen.
Horse as fleet as lightening and black as the night,
Rode past the gates on an autumn day, clean out of sight.
Minutes turned hours, hours turned into a day,
The father doesn't know her trip would be one-way.
Weeks turned into months, months turned into years,
Father died heartbroken amongst all his tears.
The fort has been abandoned, over 100 years have passed,
Every 7 years, people near here are aghast.
It is said in the distance on the same autumn day,
Look to the plains where hills and gully's sway.
Near the horizon, across the plains and out of the haze,
Her last haunting ride before her image decays.

Old House

I love abandon old houses and their stories that they tell.
Growing up in Colorado and having lived in South Dakota and
with my family roots in western Kansas I have driven by countless
old abandon farm houses and old mining shacks. The little boy in
me always wonders why they were abandoned, why the folks and
families left them to wither away in the weather and become dust
in the wind. As a young boy I would make up stories of why the
old houses were abandoned, and just like most youngsters all my
stories had a positive and happy ending. They had left for a better
life and fortune in another part of the world. As I became older and
the reality of life became known to me, I realized these abandon
old houses more likely than not had sad endings for those that had
lived there. They had become abandoned because of the misery
that life sometimes brings. Most of the time it involved the death
of the owner due to an illness or simply they died of a broken
heart. When I see one in the distance I always stop and look and
listen, sometimes I see a shadowy spectral image in the window
that has a broken pane of glass, or I hear the creak of the rotten
wooden floors as a broken hearted earthbound phantom walks the
floor forever more.

"Old House"

I look at your swayed roof, broken panes, and rotting wood,
Countless summers of heat, and winter blizzards - you have
stood.
Memories, all but forgotten smiles, tears, and countless - "I
Love You",
Laughter, sadness, and nights of love - slipped away as time
flew.
Why the people you shelter and protected left I will never
know,
Better fortunes, death, or the loneliness of the winter snow.
In your dying decay, so goes the memories that you have
stored,
From sunrise to sunset, here you sit - all alone and ignored.

Mountain Man

I feel like a man born out of time and a century or two too late, I should have been a mountain man. Growing up in the foothills of the Rocky Mountains in a time before video games, cell phones and iPads was a learning experience that kids nowadays will never know. We played outside until the sun went down and our mothers would shout out from the front steps for us to come home. Summer nights were filled with, hide and seek, and kick the can. Summer days were filled with riding your bikes, exploring the outer regions of your neighborhood and beyond with your best friends. Shooting BB guns, fishing, tubing, catching crawdads and guppies were our everyday events. More often than not we would pitch tents and camp out and watch the stars hoping to catch a shooting star. My friends and I would tell tales of ancient times of bravery and honor of those that walked our mountains before us. Our heroes were mountain men. Men like Hugh Glass, Jim Bridger, William Sublette, Jim Beckworth, and Jedediah Smith. As a youngster there were two things that changed how I would forever look at the world. The first was I read Jack London "Call of the Wild." The second was a movie starring Robert Redford "Jeremiah Johnson."

Jack London and Robert Redford cemented my love for all things wild and good ole' Mother Nature. My poem is my salute to the mountain men that dared go where no man had gone before.

"Mountain Man"

Rocky Mountains spoke to him, saying his name,
Packed his Hawkins rifle, headed there to lay his claim.
Indians fought, critters to trap, - weather to tame,
Many years passed a Mountain Man he became.
Freezing rain, bone chilling cold winter - waist deep snow,
Cold temperature and frost bite took many a toe.
Scars on his scalp from a female panther swipe,
All alone, no give up in the man - he wasn't the type.
More years passed, the harsh winters seemed longer,
Wishing for the time when he was younger and stronger.
Never once thinking about heading down below,
No way in hell - leave his loved mountain plateau.
His 50th winter, he died, gave it his all, everything he was
worth,
Living the life he chose, Rocky Mountain marrow of the earth.

"Ain't this somethin'? I told my pap and mam I was going to be a mountain man; acted like they was gut-shot. "Make your life go here, son. Here's where the people is. Them mountains is for Indians and wild men." "Mother Gue", I says "the Rocky Mountains is the marrow of the world," and by God, I was right. Keep your nose in the wind and your eye along the skyline."
Del Gue

Cowboy Gambling

Some of the old Colorado gold camps like Central City, Blackhawk, and Cripple Creek have tried to regain their former glory in recent years by legalizing gambling. Now I am not sure if that is a good thing or a bad, but one thing I do know - it has given these old former ghost towns new life and the money to rebuild. As I travel now through the mountains besides doing photography, gold panning, and ghost town hunting - I have now a new option - that is gambling. Did I mention that I am not sure if that is a bad thing or not. Maybe you can decide from reading my poem.

"*Cowboy Gambling*"

When I feel I'm packing' a heavy load of luck,
Drive to Blackhawk, Colorado in my ole' Chevy truck.
Up the mountain road to the Lodge Casino,
Play 3 card poker, Black Jack, Bonus Six - even a little Keno.
There are two women dealers I think the world of,
Oh Hell! In truth have more than grown to love.
They always make me welcome as a pat straight flush,
They kind of get this cowboy tongue tied an' starting to blush.
Julie and Tammy are the casino dealers of cards,
These two gals – I hold in the highest regards.
They're so darn purty I always feel like taking' my hat off to
them,
They have sunny smiles that make me think of a shine on
gems.
I reckon sitting at their tables – I just become enchanted,
Not paying much mind to the losing cards they just planted.
They almost always drop nothing' higher than a two-spot,
No aces, face cards or tens - not diddly squat!

Hundred dollars here, hundred dollars there,
Another losing hand, this cowboy does declare.
This old cowboy looks in his wallet to take a peek,
Sure enough, that leather holder has sprung a leak.
More than a few times that this will occur,
Luck raveled out and cleaned down to my spurs.
My cowboy gambling mind starts to ponder an' starts dwell,
That I had about as much chance as a wax cat in hell.
If you have read this sorry poem - it may appear,
That this cowboy maybe plumb weak north of the ears.
Now I will tell in this tale known only to a few,
Any amount of money is worth sitting at a table with these
two.
Even thou I may need a Doc that does skull practice,
I'm always left grinning' like a jackass eating' cactus.

*"Guessing has never been
widely acclaimed
as a good gambling strategy."*
Unknown Author

John Muir

When I travel the Rocky Mountains or any wilderness trail – I think of John Muir, even though most of his work and writings were even further west than Colorado. His writings and descriptions of the mountains and of wilderness areas have always left me wanting more. John Muir the naturalist was a man that inspired me with his thoughts and deeds – sometimes I feel him standing over my shoulder talking to me when I read what he left behind – like it was written just for me. I have been asked before if by a quirk of fate and I could talk to one person now deceased. Who would that be? Without hesitation that person would be John Muir.

"John Muir"

Ascending high in the Rocky Mountains – if I listen I will
hear,
The voice of John Muir – sometimes far away, sometimes
near.
Muir knew of the tug, and pulling of the heart and soul,
Because of him – wandering the mountains, I must stroll.
He knew of the mountain music and wrote of its lovely tune,
He saw the beauty of the remote mountain high – under a full
moon.
The quaking of the aspens – He would listen silently and
wonder,
He would also marvel at the mountain storms of lightning and
thunder.
To hear his call and be able to walk his footsteps, I have been
blessed,
John Muir – words of nature inspired me in my own
wilderness quest,
Before me he felt – the peaceful longing, the sense of serenity,
Just like Muir – the Rockies have become a part of my
identity.
The wilderness quote that inspires me – belongs to John Muir,
He understood the remote mountains and its magical lure.
Walking John Muir's path of the white capped shrouds of so
long ago,
His words travel with me – "The Mountains are calling and I
must go"

Blame it on Willie and Waylon

Each and every one of us has a musical soundtrack just like a moving picture show. Music and what we listen to - in most ways define this condition we call human. Songs we listened to from our past bring forth memories of our youth. This personal soundtrack will make you smile, cry, and make your heart flutter to the beat of being young again. In my youth growing up In Colorado it was outlaw country and the kings of outlaw country were Waylon Jennings and Willie Nelson. For those that may not be familiar with this brand of music it was popular in the 70's and early 80's and had its roots in Honky Tonk and Rockabilly with a blend of rock and folk rhythms. My music is my escape and if the music every stopped so would time itself. It would be inconceivable.

"Blame it on Willie and Waylon"

Outlaw country was the music of my wandering youth,
Willie and Waylon were my heroes – that's the truth.
My traveling music was all the sad songs and back beat,
Nothing finer than Honky Tonk and Rockabilly – nothing that
sweet.
Had KC lights and a roll bar on my "67"- F-100 Ford,
Lift kit, cassette player and more than a few dents - it was all I
could afford.
Had all the cassettes of Willie, Waylon, and Johnny Cash,
Lost Merle Haggard, David Allan Coe as they melted on my
pickup dash.
All my friends listened to the outlaw Honky Tonk music back
in the day,
Bonfires On the banks of the South Platte River we drank and
sometimes it got a little risqué.
We drank Peppermint Schnapps, Coors Light the Silver Bullet
beer,
We were young, invincible with nothing at all to fear.

When the mountains called Kellie Shawn and I would head
that way,
Listen to Tanya Tucker, Hank Williams Jr. as we 4-wheeled to
our hidden getaway.
Kellie Shawn was my girl and she set my body on fire,
With Jessi Colter, Tompall Glaser on the radio – we gave into
our hearts desire.
Anything I did - that I am sorry for back when I was young,
I can blame it on Willie and Waylon and the songs they sung.
As I have grown older and sometimes get down feeling life's
pain,
I plug in Willie Nelsons - "Blue eyes crying in the rain."
From time to time I think of those days and get lonesome in
my soul,
Then I listen to Willie, and Waylon, - down memory lane I
start to stroll.

"I may be crazy, but it keeps me from going insane."
Waylon Jennings

Midnight Wind

What I like is a Colorado Rocky Mountain night when you step away from the flickering and dancing campfire light into the darkness of the night. In the nocturnal dimness if you listen closely the forest and the trees are an orchestra with the midnight wind as the maestro. The pitch of the songs they sing changes with the quickness of the wind. Most folks never step away from the safety and comfort of the campfire and they miss the mountain songs that are sung by the wind. I feel sad for those that stay in the light and never hear this healing melody.

"Midnight Wind"

Climb the Rocky Mountains and listen, in the distance you will hear.
The song of the wilderness midnight wind as it gathers – drawing near.
Out of the north when the day becomes night – the wind sends its legacy.
Aspen leaves become the instrument for the midnight song and its melody.
Mountain aspens and evergreen trees start to sway – begin to sing.
Each night the midnight wind resonates – the song and its familiar ring.
Stop and stand still and eavesdrop – hold out your arms, face the sky,
With your eyes close, slowly turn and open your spirit – don't ask why.
In our lives we have the peaks and the valleys on the trail we have taken,
When we have despair – midnight wind repairs the soul and helps it reawaken.
Out of the north the midnight wind has a healing song – a tale for you.
The wind if you listen and take heed – essence, mind and body, start to renew.

Just remember, when your soul and spirit is down and nothing
seems right,
Climb a mountain – turn your face to the sky, feel the midnight
winds might.
In the mountains – when darkness descent's and the wind builds
– do not be afraid.
For in the night you will hear the midnight wind, its song – your
happiness remade.
Climb the Rocky Mountains and listen, in the distance you will
hear.
The song of the wilderness midnight wind as it gathers –
drawing near.

*"I still get wildly enthusiastic about little things... I play with
leaves. I skip down the street and run against the wind."*
Leo Buscaglia

Grumpy's Bear

I use to live near Grand Lake, Colorado which is about 9,000 feet in altitude and the gateway into Rocky Mountain National Park and some of the most remote wilderness areas in Colorado. Grumpy's is a saloon on Main Street that I use to partake in a cold beverage from time to time. The beginning of this poem and tale is true and the rest maybe – not so true.

"Grumpy's Bear"

One summer night in Grumpy's Saloon in Colorado – town of
Grand Lake,
Nursing a couple of beers – when walked in a bear for
goodness sake.
He appeared out of the darkness and strolled through an open
back door,
Jake, Eddie and I were in disbelief and hoping there weren't
any more.
We were staring when Jake pointed and stuttered, "Do you see
the damn bear?"
Slowly shaking my head – I gasped, "I am not blind Jake – I
see him over there!"
Now Grand Lake is near timberline in the mountains with
bears all around,
My buddies and I – never heard of a tale in a saloon – one had
ever been found.
Now this here bear was one magnificent and powerful looking
fellow,
For the moment it would seem he was just curious and very
mellow.

Then he spied a beer on the other side of the bar and reached
for the can,
Raising my eyebrows and a little disgusted – I was never a
Budweiser fan.
With one colossal swipe – he split that can wide open and
spilled all the beer,
He started to slap his huge paws on the bar – giving us
something to fear.
With a valiant roar the 800 pound bear looked at me drinking
my cold Coors lite,
Thinking now if that bear went for my Coors it was going to
be one hell of a fight.
Jake and Eddie were terrified when Eddie muttered, "Hurry
boys to the pickup!"
Dammit- Grumpy's was our bar – "Stand your ground boys
now is the time too – Cowboy Up!"
Thinking – there never was a horse that couldn't be rode or a
bear that couldn't be beat,
Pointing at the bear, "You better settle your furry ass down
and get lost or take a seat!"
That mammoth bears simple mind you could see the wheels
and gears were spinning,
As Jake, Eddie and I with Coors lite in hands and now the 3 of
us – all were grinning.
That bear now pondered and deciphered that the boys and I
had grown a pair,
Out – the open back door whence he came – into the darkness
went Grumpy's Bear.

*Colorado is my home - I love the mountains and the wilderness -
living anywhere else is not acceptable.*
Kurt James

About The Author

Kurt James was born and raised in the foothills of the Colorado Rocky Mountains. With family roots in western Kansas and having lived in South Dakota for 20 years Kurt James naturally had become an old western and nature enthusiast. Over the years Kurt James has become one of Colorado's prominent nature photographer's through his brand name of Midnight Wind Photography. His poetry has been featured in the Denver Post, PM Magazine and on 9NEWS in Denver, Colorado. Kurt is also a feature writer for Hubpages and Creative Exiles with the article's focused on Colorado history, ghost towns, outlaws, and poetry. Inspired at a young age by writers such as Jack London, Louis L'Amour and Max Brand have formed Kurt's natural ability as a story teller. Kurt James "Rocky Mountain" historical fiction series of 3 books that provide western adventure of the early days of the Rocky Mountain frontier and his newly released "Thoughts and Poetry of a Wandering Man" - the (Uniquely Colorado edition) are available in print and download on Amazon, Barnes and Noble, Goodreads and other fine bookstores. And a few shady bookstores as well. Kurt is currently working on his 4th historical fiction novel "The Keegan Trail".

KJ

KURT JAMES AUTHOR

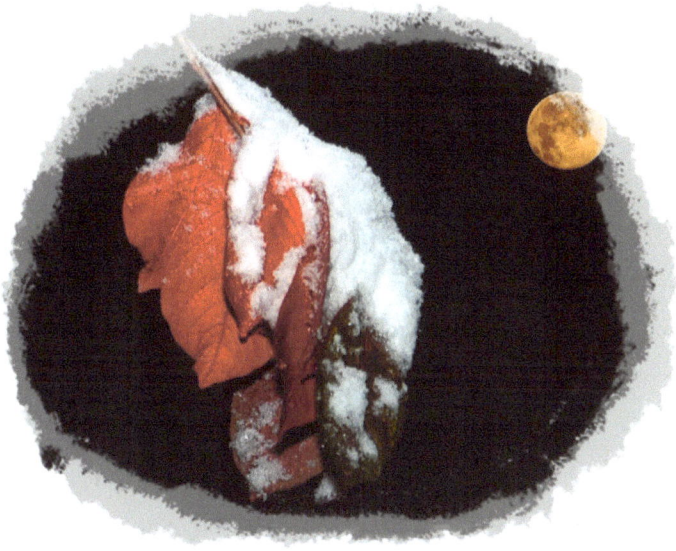

Kurt James